Loving thoughts as your child leaves the nest...

Fly Away

Eme Mc Anam

This book is
dedicated to Alan

Greetings, Dear Friends,

I've loved being a mother. As my son embarked on his own path, I experienced a mix of emotions - mourning the departure while also celebrating his new journey. This phase, often termed as preparing for the empty nest, marked a significant transition in my life. As a longtime singer-songwriter, I poured my sentiments into lyrics, crafting "Fly Away" to encapsulate my experience. Since then, I've shared this song in various settings, including a heartfelt rendition at my son's grooms' dinner and a symbolic performance as an 'eagle woman' in 2016.

I've found that "Fly Away" touches the hearts of others navigating significant life passages. I share this reminder that in our moments of transition, we're not alone.

It's my hope that the lyrics of "Fly Away" serve as a source of solace and encouragement during those pivotal moments in life.

With warm regards,

Eme

Preparing us both
For future goodbye.

That I will help you go

I trust you are ready
For the life
you will know.

Fly away!

Celebrate life

You're ready to go

Take my love in flight.

I feathered the nest Before I brought you home

I'm glad to be part of Preparing you for more.

My nest is empty
Who will I be?

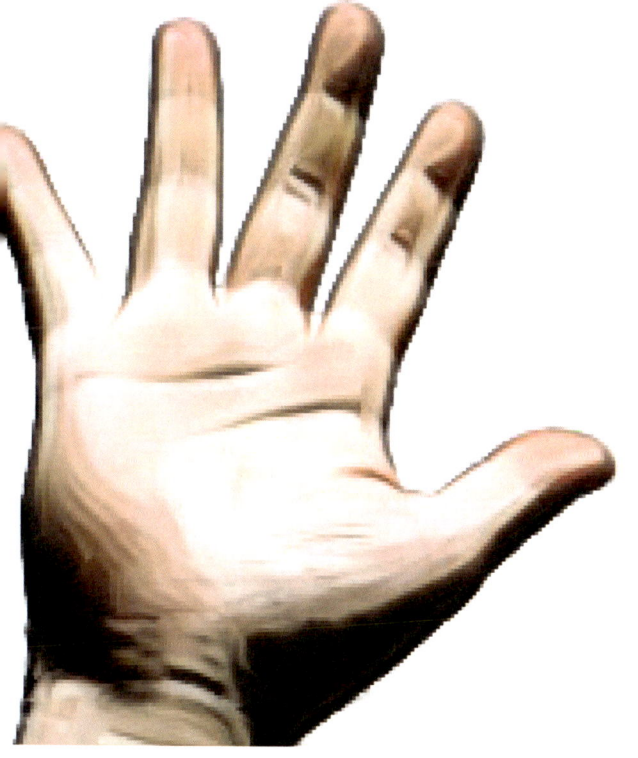
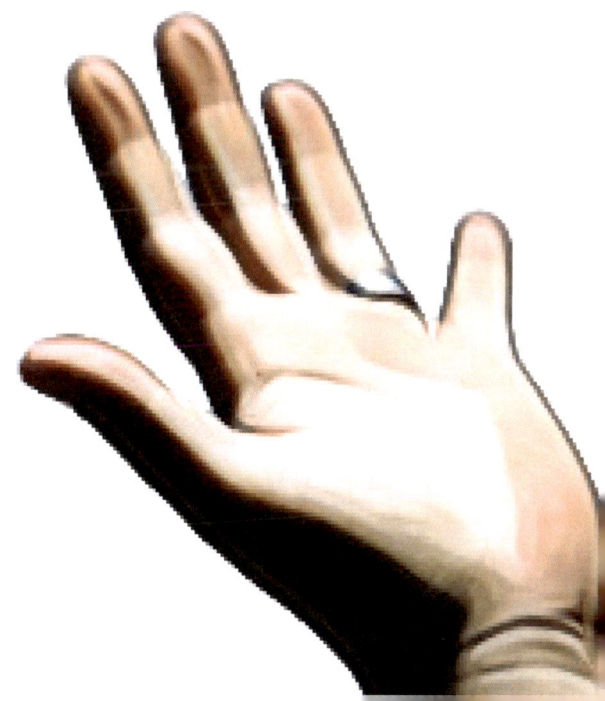

It's all in God's hands now

As I say goodbye.

Fly away!

Come back

in spring

Tell of your journey

The joy it brings

Fly Away

Copyright © 2024 by Eme Mc Anam

All rights reserved. No part of this book may be reproduced or transmitted in any form or by any means, electronic or mechanical, including photocopying, recording, or by any information storage and retrieval system, without permission in writing from the author, except for brief quotations in critical articles, books, or reviews.

CONNECT WITH Eme Mc Anam
Facebook: EmeSpirit
Instagram: EmeSpirit
Website: EmeSpirit.com

Your support and respect for the author's creative work are greatly appreciated. Thank you for purchasing *Fly Away*.

contact info@AutumnStoriesPublishing for more information

Fly Away lyrics and melody by Eme
Youtube vocal performance video: https://www.youtube.com/watch?v=oYa6fHUW1EQ

Design Layout by WOTB Designs

www.ingramcontent.com/pod-product-compliance
Lightning Source LLC
Chambersburg PA
CBRC091210010526
44119CB00020B/367